Audition Repertoire for the Advancing Pianist

Two Stylistically Balanced & Technically Diverse Programs | Edited by Jane Magrath

ISBN-10: 0-7390-5893-2
ISBN-13: 978-0-7390-5893-0

Alfred

The selections in this book are intended to provide music for the advancing pianist that is motivating and balanced in terms of period contrast and style. The pieces are "tried and true" selections—piano works that have formed the basis of audition repertoire throughout the 20th and into the 21st centuries. For many years, performers at this level have enjoyed playing these pieces, which have become standards in the lower-advanced piano repertoire. I am sure that you'll find some of your favorites included here.

Audition Repertoire for the Advancing Pianist, Book 2 contains two programs from which to choose to create a well-balanced audition, festival or recital program. Note the variety of composers, moods and musical characters within the pieces in each program. Most individuals will study one of the programs within a semester of piano study. Some individuals may work longer on the pieces, but it is best to choose a program that can be mastered within approximately one academic semester. Some may want to mix compositions between the two programs (however, note that the programs as presented are designed to be balanced).

To best learn these compositions, avoid practicing at a very slow tempo for too long. While slow practice of individual passages is desirable and necessary, a composition that is played under-tempo daily for too long (more than four to six weeks) may grow stale. In this case, the performer could lose his or her innate instinct for the underlying character of the work. It is also suggested that the performer memorize the pieces as early as possible. Please take time to study the editorial commentary on the scores (see page 3).

I hope that you derive as much pleasure from practicing and playing this music as I have. You are delving into the great art-literature for our instrument—what a great privilege and challenge!

Warm thanks and sincere appreciation to Morty and Iris Manus, Tom Gerou, Carol Matz and E. L. Lancaster for their support and help with this series.

A Special Note to the Performer

These pieces have been selected with the performer and his or her enrichment in mind. Best wishes for many days of delight, joy and beauty as you practice and perform these selections. Most importantly, learn to critique yourself by listening carefully as you play (be your own teacher while practicing), and enjoy every piece that you read or study!

Jane Magrath

Editorial Commentary

Sinfonia No. 11 in G Minor, BWV 797 (Bach)

All parenthetical material and fingerings are editorial. The primary touch is legato throughout. You may use pedal in this piece, but sparingly. For this beautiful, lyrical melody, the performer needs a rich singing tone in the long musical ideas. The *Sinfonias* are challenging works that might be regarded as fugue-like, although the first announcement of the theme is accompanied by counterpoint.

Bach's works brought Baroque music to its highest perfection; for this reason, most historians date the end of the era with his death in 1750. Bach's family played a significant role in German music for over 150 years.

Sonata in E Major, Op. 14, No. 1 (Third Movement) (Beethoven)

All parenthetical material and fingerings are editorial. Note the sudden changes of dynamics in this piece, created intentionally to surprise the listeners and create humor. Be careful not to over-pedal in measures 47–83. A light accent pedal on the staccato bass octaves in this section may be appropriate. This rondo sparkles with rapid scales and broken chords. Be sure to convey a lilting, spontaneous and refreshing spirit as you play.

Beethoven was a musical giant who, by the time he was 30, became one of the most renowned pianists and composers in Europe. Although he adhered to Classical forms, his music was highly innovative from the beginning stages of his composing.

Grillen ("Whims") (from Fantasiestücke), Op. 12, No. 4 (Schumann)

All parenthetical material and fingerings are editorial. This piece is humorous and capricious, filled with a whirlwind of successive ideas. The original score is marked "Pedal" at measure 1. A general marking such as this is usually interpreted as an indication to use pedal throughout the piece as needed, in the opinion of the performer and in conjunction with the performance practice precepts for the composer and style. Here, the editor suggests using accent pedals in measures 1, 3, 4–6, etc. Avoid pedaling through the many staccato chords, since they help create the humor and energy in the music.

The piece is in sonata rondo form (**A B A C A B**[1] **A**). The melody should project at the start of the **C** section (measure 61). The grace notes in measure 87 should be played slowly, as a rolled chord, and pedal should be held from this rolled figure through the fermata in measure 88.

Schumann's creative, fanciful mind has produced some of the most imaginative music in the piano repertoire. His music was influenced by his strong literary background (his father was a bookseller). Schumann wrote plays and poems, and founded a progressive journal that was critical of salon music and musical stagnation.

Clair de lune (from Suite bergamasque) (Debussy)

All parenthetical material and fingerings are editorial. This piece may have been inspired by Verlaine's poem "Clair de lune" (Moonlight). Note the composer's respect and reverence for the beauty of moonlight with all of its magic and shimmer. Pedal should be used throughout much of this piece, with pedal changes usually occurring with changes in harmony (signaled by a left-hand chord change). Some scholars advocate the use of the *sostenuto* pedal in measures 15–24.

Be sure to maintain a steady pulse (musical "heartbeat") throughout the performance of this work, since it can become easy to play freely. An increase in musical intensity accompanied by a slight increase in tempo should occur at measures 27–43. Be careful not to exaggerate any rubato passages. Pay careful attention to voicing, color, rhythmic accuracy and the many expression markings in the score. Debussy composed three pieces with the title "Clair de lune" in his lifetime—two songs and this piano piece.

Sonata in C Major, K. 159; L. 104 (Scarlatti)

All fingerings and dynamics are editorial. Articulation markings, given as examples of suggested articulation for similar passages throughout, are also editorial. Some editions omit measure 16. Notice the simulated horn calls in the opening, the presence of ornaments suggesting castanets, and some "Spanish rhythms." Opportunities to play echo effects can be found in various passages, such as measures 1–4 and 27–30, but the performer should be careful not to overuse this technique. This is one of the best-known Scarlatti sonatas.

Sonata in F Minor, Op. 2, No. 1 (First Movement) (Beethoven)

All parenthetical material and fingerings are editorial. Notice the "rocket" theme—an ascending arpeggio—that opens the movement. This is a gesture that had formerly been used by a group of composers from Mannheim, Germany. Beethoven uses drama throughout the movement, often by frequent use of accents such as *sforzandi* and accents on weak beats. Notice the places where Beethoven pauses the music (measures 8 and 108) and leaves the listener in suspense. Pedal sparingly in this work. Where a choice exists, it is preferable to change the pedal too frequently rather than not often enough.

Waltz in E Minor, KK IVa, No. 15 (Op. Posth.) (Chopin)

All parenthetical material and fingerings are editorial. "KK" stands for Krystina Koblyanska's thematic catalog of Chopin's works. Some performers begin the rolled chords in measures 3, 4, 5, etc. simultaneously with the last eighth note pulse of the prior measure. The ornament in measure 11 should be played quickly before the beat, due to the tempo of this piece. The flourish in measures 125-126 may be divided between the hands. The pedal indications are original with Chopin (except for those in parentheses) but beware that not all of these indications may be satisfactory on the modern piano. Performers may need to make adjustments in measures 59–60, 67–68 and 113–116, as well as in other places. Remember that additional pedal may be used. This waltz is effective and brilliant in performance, but needs a fluid right-hand technique.

Chopin was one of the few truly great composers to achieve distinction solely by writing piano music. Even during his lifetime, the popularity of some of his mazurkas, waltzes, nocturnes and polonaises brought Chopin great fame.

Sonatine (Second Movement) (Ravel)

All fingerings are editorial. This second movement of Ravel's three-movement *Sonatine* features a typical minuet rhythm and often has an accented or prolonged second beat. One pedal per measure is appropriate in measures 17–21, 25, 39–40 and 69–77, while longer pedals may be needed beginning in measures 13, 23 and 79. More frequent pedal changes can occur in measures 4, 6–11 and 16. The technique of "half pedaling," or bringing the pedal only halfway up to a "half-muted" stage, can be employed in this piece on some pianos and in some halls to further refine the sonorities.

Sonatine was written for a competition held by a local magazine. In some ways, the work shows Ravel's tendencies towards writing in more traditional forms. The piece as a whole represents Ravel's neoclassicism at its best.

Sinfonia No. 11 in G Minor

Johann Sebastian Bach (1685–1750)
BWV 797

Sonata in E Major
(Third Movement)

Ludwig van Beethoven (1770–1827)
Op. 14, No. 1

12

Grillen
("Whims")
from *Fantasiestücke*

Robert Schumann (1810–1856)
Op. 12, No. 4

Clair de lune
(from *Suite bergamasque*)

Claude Debussy (1862–1918)

20

22

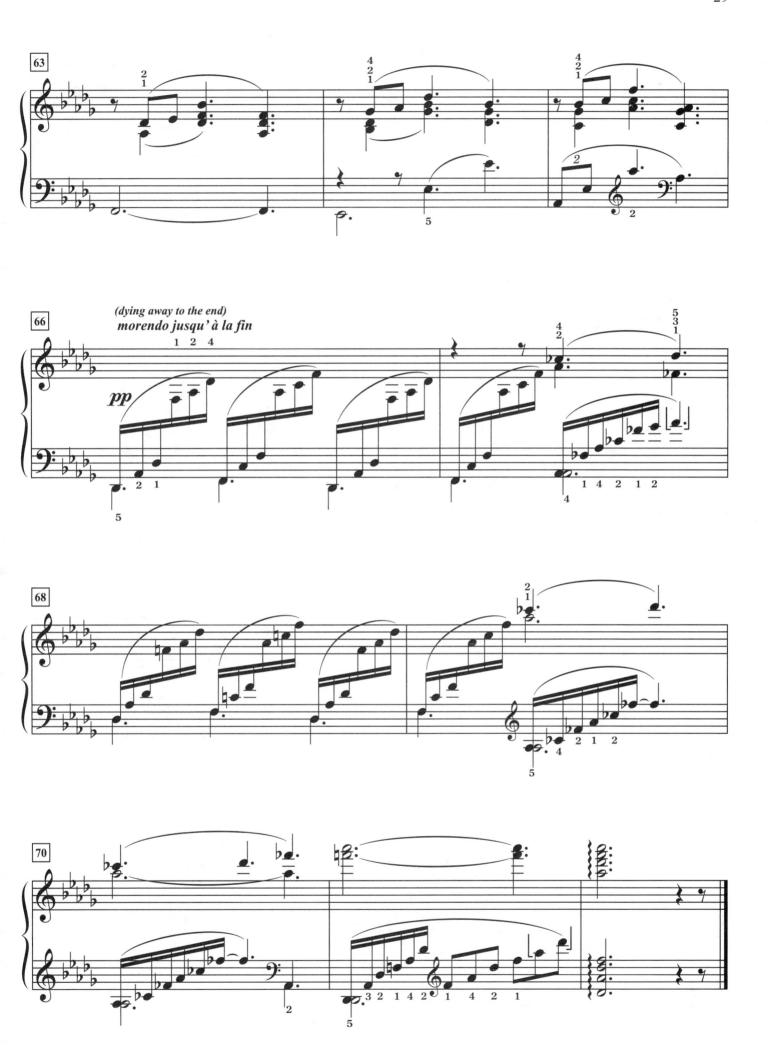

(dying away to the end)
morendo jusqu' à la fin

Sonata in C Major

Domenico Scarlatti (1685–1757)
K. 159; L. 104

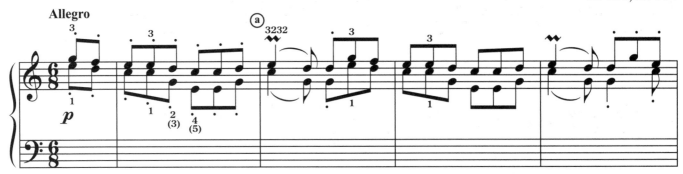

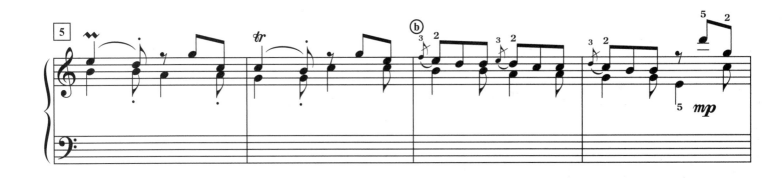

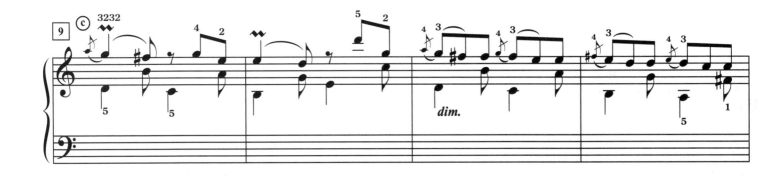

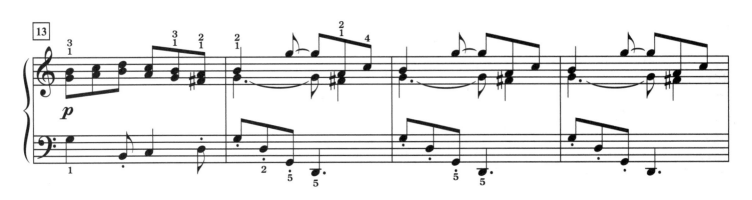

Sonata in F Minor
(First Movement)

Ludwig van Beethoven (1770–1827)
Op. 2, No. 1

(d) A redistribution similar to footnote (b) is possible here.

Waltz in E Minor
KK IVa, No. 15

Frédéric Chopin (1810–1849)
Op. Posth.

Sonatine
(Second Movement)

Maurice Ravel (1875–1937)

ⓐ The unconnected "ties" are an indication to let the notes ring.

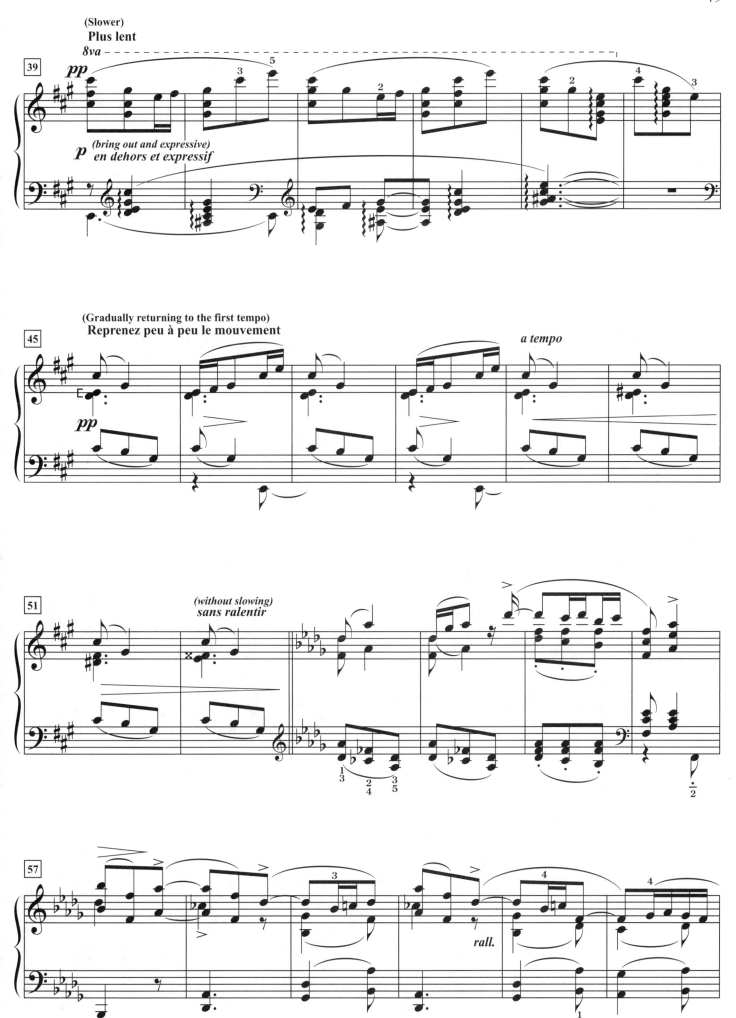